CRITTER TALES

Adventures in Rehabilitating Wildlife

Author – John Russ
Cover Images – April Russ
Photography – April Russ
Aerial Photography – Rob Banton
Background Images – Simpson Point Press
Design and Editing – Simpson Point Press

Shamballa Wildlife Rescue is a 501(c)(3) non-profit
dedicated to the rescue, rehab and release of Alabama wildlife.

Shamballa Wildlife Rescue is licensed by the state of Alabama.
We cover Jackson and Marshall Counties in North Alabama.

Critter Tales may be purchased in bulk
for fundraising and retail sales.
For information, please contact the publisher or
Shamballa Wildlife Rescue
4268 Cathedral Caverns Road
Woodville, Alabama 35776
www.facebook.com/Shamballawildliferescue

Published by Simpson Point Press • P.O. Box 205 • Grant, Alabama 35747
www.simpsonpointpress.com • moreaboutthat@gmail.com

Dedication and Acknowledgements

I dedicate this to my best friend, wife and soul mate April, who understands everything. Her love and encouragement inspire me daily. This book is her adventure, too, and I wouldn't want it any other way.

I also dedicate this book to the memory of April's father **Marcel Moreau**, whose wisdom still guides us today.

In my life I have been extremely lucky. I have cared for, been cared for, and been loved by some gems of the human race. This is a feeble attempt to acknowledge just a few of them…

Thank you to my dear friends: **Steve and Kathy Coon** whose priceless care and encouragement have given me the confidence to "jump on in" and try anything (so here I am); **Ron and Katie Bilton** who taught me about trust and the simple fun of laughter with good friends. Neither time, distance, nor end of life has dimmed their friendship and generous support of our cause; **Rob and LoriAnn Banton** for their assistance over the years with raising babies, providing release sites and so much more; **Keith Daniel** for the ingenious workmanship that has saved us so much time and effort; **Valerie Leonard** for her continuous support and dear companionship; **Valerie and Rich Krumrie** for their undying support and friendship; **Herb Neu and Sasha Reynolds** who made this book possible through their hard work, encouragement and professionalism; and **all our neighbors** for their constant support and kindness.

And of course, all those through the years who have donated and supported our cause, both in our local community and our followers online, we thank you deeply.

The Meaning of Shamballa

In Tibetan Buddhist lore, the word Shamballa refers to a mythical kingdom of enlightenment and peace. The key to paradise is within, and all around us, it suggests. Shamballa exemplifies kindness, compassion and, most of all, harmony with nature.

When we moved to our little cabin, on the front lawn stood a lonely cedar tree, so old and yet so strong. April fell in love with the tree. She gave it a face and named it the Shamballa Tree.

It has survived storms and heavy snow. It has withstood flooding and outlasted drought. It is the oldest tree in this neighborhood. Every year it provides shelter to countless humming-bird nests. A family of blue birds nest in the little cabin hung from its branches. Horses and goats shelter in its shade from the hot summer sun.

Our Shamballa Tree reminds us to strive for understanding, care and benevolence.

Contents

Prologue

This adventure really started when we bought our little dream log cabin in North Alabama, outside Woodville, a small rural town of less than 750 people, mostly farmers and retirees. Woodville boasts of being the first town in Jackson County, although there's not even a town square, only a vintage barber shop that I've never seen open, a welding shop, and the railroad track that runs smack through the middle of town. One small white gazebo marks the city's center.

In the abundant forests of the hills and valleys surrounding Woodville, and other nearby towns, tall cedars, red and white oaks, persimmon, and many other trees form a beautiful cloud-like green curtain, concealing just how deep the woods really are. A daily stroll into these forests—forest bathing some call it—will free you of any tensions you may have had upon entering. Situated in the lower foothills of the Appalachian Mountains, we enjoy four seasons, from eye-popping spring flowers to winters so cold our eyes burn.

My charming wife April was born in Brussels, Belgium, and she is totally fascinated by the wildlife here in Alabama, especially raccoons. And deer. And opossums. And more. April has a tremendous way with animals, especially wild ones. They love her back. She has a gift.

When we first began our quest to become full-fledged, licensed Wildlife Rehabilitators, the idea of rehabbing and releasing wild animals back into their natural habitat sounded so appealing. And once we recovered from the "adventure" that obtaining our permit was, it has been a priceless journey.

However, I must say here that rehabbing is not for everyone. It can be extremely

stressful, especially if you tend to get too attached to the creatures. Some die for no apparent reason, some will never like you and some, despite your best efforts, will die of wounds you have tried so hard to mend. We have a small plot out back with an assortment of memorial crosses, plaques and headstones as warm reminders of the ones that didn't make it but live on in our memory.

Letting go of any animal, pet or otherwise, that you have cared for and come to know is hard enough when they die. But to walk out into the woods, open that carrier door and voluntarily release this self-sufficient, healthy critter that you just realized you love, THAT is tough!

Eventually though, your outlook changes and you begin to see the other side of what *rehabbers*, as we are collectively known, do. We are stewards; we try to assist nature. Hopefully, years from now, we may walk a path and meet, face to face, a direct relative of one of our charges. This thought makes opening that carrier door little easier for me.

Story 1

Raccoon Favorites

The orphaned animals we receive come from many different situations. We try to communicate to the finder that the best scenario, if possible, is to simply return the baby close by where it was found. An animal mom may roam pretty far away in search of food, but be assured she will return in the evening to reclaim and nurse her offspring. An abandoned fawn lying low in the grass is NOT necessarily an orphan. Mom has simply wandered off to forage or has been frightened by you.

Of all the reasons orphaned babies end up with us, the mom being hit by a car is by far the most common. Attacks by dogs, cats and coyotes also take their toll on wild moms, as well as their babies. Our goal is simply to assist nature in caring for her creations.

Our first attempt at rehabbing four orphaned raccoons, approximately three weeks old, was encouraging and successful. We converted a portable dog kennel into their home. With added swings, ropes and a water-filled, tiny plastic foot tub, the kits, as young raccoons are known, were seldom bored. April learned to bottle feed them by online research, instinct, seminars and a tremendous amount of trial and error. And she discovered that different babies sometimes need different styles of *mothering*. One may need the top of his head rubbed while feeding, another may need to hold onto her finger.

After their formula is gradually replaced with soft-solid foods, they are slowly weaned and ready for some outdoor fun. Keep in mind that each baby is individual, so this weaning may take a week to ten days, even longer in some species. During this time, the baby's eyes will open, and it will become fully furred.

We teach the baby raccoons to fish by dropping several ice cubes into their play pool, which is a child's plastic wading pool. After several days and when the little ones can grasp the ice for a bite, we go to our local bait shop, buy a dozen minnows and substitute these for the ice. After they finally settle down, most likely soaked from fishing, they will eventually get it. We then skip their normal meal that day. By leaving them hungry, they will feel the need to eat the fish. Otherwise, they just play, biting the head off and leaving it to rot. Dead fish is an unpleasantly stinky cleaning job.

This *fishing* lesson, besides teaching coordination, gives them their first taste of live food. Amazing, huh? When you think about it, it's only common sense. Still, a brilliant technique.

As soon as they are weaned, we feed them only in the evening. The food will be left there all night and any leftovers are cleaned in the morning and the water freshened up. By having them active and eating and playing in the evening, we get them used to being more nocturnal. They usually relax and sleep all day during the hot hours, with a dip in the pool every now and again to cool down.

Releasing our first raccoon rehabs, Zorro, Gem, Blizzard and Steve, was tough on both of us. Bittersweet, but mostly bitter. After a long drive into the remote

land where a friend had permitted us to release rehabilitated animals, we placed the carrier next to a stream, lined by heavy woods. April opened the carrier door and Blizzard warily peeked out, then slowly slunk out and sniffed the air. Spying the stream, he waddled down, nose twitching madly, stopped and looked back at us. Neither of us had a dry eye.

We quietly repeated this release three more times that day and each of them was as precious as the last. Looking back, these four orphaned raccoons taught us much more than we taught them.

Since then, we still learn every year and the lessons are always different. We expanded by adapting three ten-foot-square dog kennels into more raccoon housing. Each has a large, cozy shelter box and can be closed in case of bad weather or to contain critters during enclosure scrubbing. Raccoons simply cannot resist a moving and clattering rake, so unless you have half a day to dodge and wrestle with them, it is a better idea to simply lock them in their shelter box for a few minutes during cleaning time.

From previous experiences, we have found that, across the board, all wild

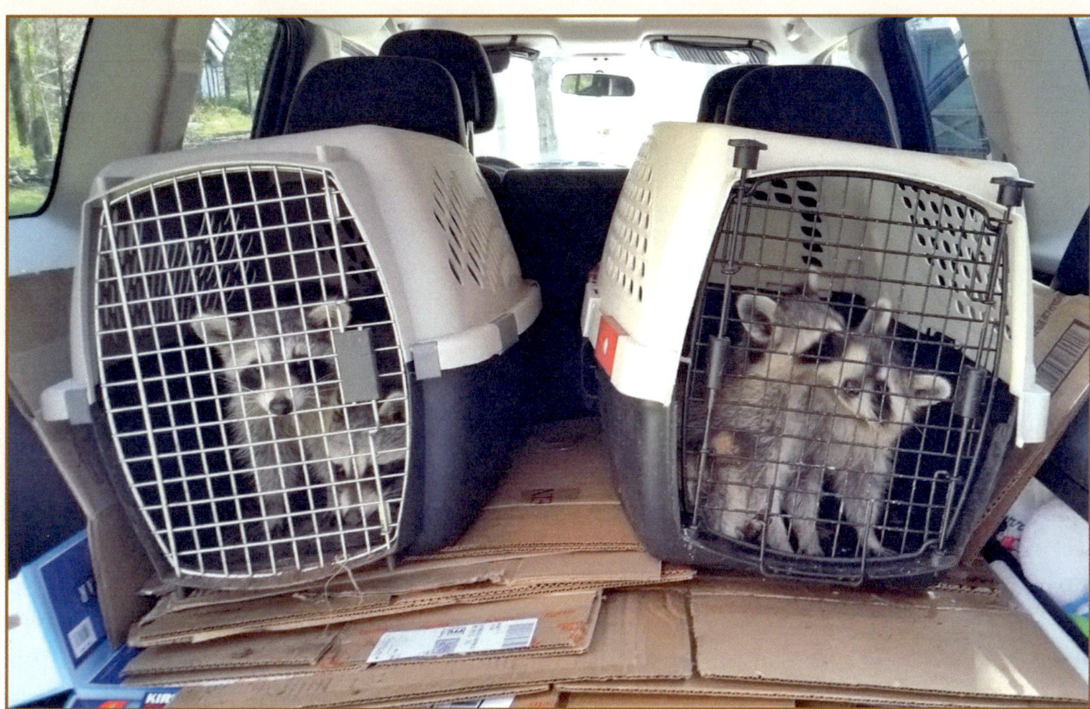

animals thrive when their enclosure contains "enrichment" elements. These can be as simple as a plastic ball, even a tree limb propped against the enclosure wall. Or, depending on your imagination and carpentry skills, an old ATV tire suspended on a rope about eight inches off the floor. Items with the feel of fur and that squeak or pop supply babies with hours of exercise and entertainment. Let your imagination run wild. April shops yard sales, thrift stores and such for any stuffed toys, teething rings and even feather boas, any inexpensive prize that can safely be used to entertain her critters. Tree limbs propped up at an angle so they can climb, slide, fall and generally wear their little bodies out, seem to make them happier raccoons.

Let's not forget about hammocks. April has designed a simple blanket that is spread out just below the roof of the enclosure and suspended by bungee cords on all four corners. Raccoons use this to jump, wrestle, chew and for napping during the heat of the day. The springiness of it seems appealing and they lounge in it for hours.

As I write this, I am watching a two-month-old raccoon we call Wanda terrorize a ping-pong ball inside a plastic feed dish. The more it rattles, the better she likes it. We have a saying between April and me: "If you're bored, it's your own darn fault." Enrichment is only limited by our imaginations. It works as a priceless tool for assuring healthy, releasable wildlife.

There are many more tips we have discovered and some of them must be shared in context. Otherwise this is just an instructional manual—which it is *not* meant to be. This is supposed to be an adventure—so let's adventure!

Story 2

Fawn Favorites

Delilah

There is no doubt in my mind which animal was, and is, my all-time favorite… our first rescue.

The little fawn was picked up beside a busy highway in Stevenson, Alabama. She was healthy but traumatized and weighed four pounds. We estimated her age at approximately two weeks. Her large ears were straight (curly ears are an early sign of dehydration). A sweet young couple had found her next to her Mom, who had died crossing the road. She bonded with April immediately and cooperated in every way, once she was with us for a few days. For feeding convenience, we kept her in the nursery, a converted storage building close behind our house. Her name just came to us and fit her perfectly, Delilah, Dee for short.

After just a few days with us, she was transferred to the large outdoor enclosure. We constructed a chain link pen, fifty feet by fifty feet for white-tailed deer fawns. Here she could stretch her long, thin legs and exercise to her heart's content. One of my favorite pastimes was watching Dee sprint around at full speed, gracefully bounding over rocks and logs, her spots just blurs. This little doe was adapting very nicely to her temporary home.

During the next two months, we acquired two more fawns, both victims of road accidents, one with a broken front leg, which was splinted by our local veterinarian. But our first, Delilah, stood out. She was

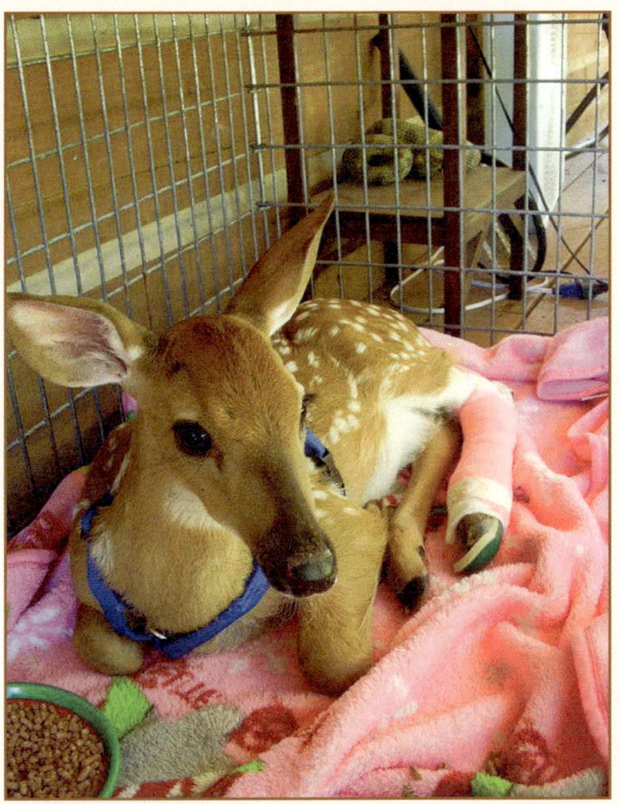

gentle, trusting and a devoted sis to her adopted sisters.

April bottle fed Delilah and her sisters powdered formula, often enduring the ninety-degree-plus weather at feeding time. Dee and the other fawns all thrived.

There is a tune April whistles while walking out to the deer run. The tune is a Christmas carol. Yes, there is a reason (I asked). She claims that this song is so out of season now, that no one could entice her fawns to come to them unless they were familiar and harmless…and what better way to say, "I'm safe, I'm harmless"… than a song? One more part of her magic, I guess.

Delilah and her sister without the cast were eventually let out

of the run and allowed to graze and forage during the day. It was a real joy to watch them run, jump, and twirl, enjoying this new unrestricted freedom.

We made a small outdoor firepit *gathering spot* on the back of our land and April has dubbed it her "Prayer Place." The trees around it are thick. As we sat on log benches one cool summer evening, I asked April what she had learned from Delilah.

Delilah's instincts were excellent from the start, she reflected. *I used to follow her in the woods to see what she was eating, so I could bring the right browsing material back to the other doe who had a broken leg (Macy). So I learned to provide the right foraging for any fawn who couldn't get to the forest because of health issues. If the baby could not get to the forest yet, then I would bring the forest to it. Delilah was my teacher and my guide.*

At dusk April would walk out to the run, whistling her Christmas carol, and the ladies would trot up to her for an evening bottle and solid treats. Deer adore most cookies and these, along with fruits, enticed them back into the run at night. We do not have a major problem with predators, but just in case, we house them at night.

One evening during feeding, April discovered a large notch in Delilah's right ear. Apparently, she had torn it foraging during the day. April cleaned and disinfected it and eventually the notch healed but never grew back together. So, this became her *trademark,* a sure-fire way to identify Dee from a distance and from other does.

There comes that time when every fawn must begin explorations and adventures of their own. After about three months, we left less and less fruit, corn and treats out back for these three as they became independent. Once in awhile, after they had gone on their own, all three would show up for a visit and their growth always amazed me. The white spots disappear gradually and their coats may turn a dull gray, at other times a rusty red. Sadly, as winter set in, our

fawns visited less and less. The occasional visits were and are a highlight of our winter days. Dee and her sisters roam the two small mountains and the hollow where we live. They would appear like shadows in the evening, twitching tails and ears, missing not a sound, not a movement. Grazing on the sweet grass

and wild persimmons dropped from the trees, the small herd they were a part of moved silently across our view. Then, as quietly as they had appeared, they slipped invisibly back into the opposite stand of cedars.

One spring morning, the third year that Dee came around after she'd returned to the wild, as we were bottle feeding the new group of fawns, April looked up and there she was. Our dogs were with us and Dee had seen them before. She was alertly standing beside a small stand of trees behind the house. Our Rottweiler mix, Dixie, was sniffing the ground and wandered close to the trees. Suddenly Dee's ears dropped and she darted between Dixie and the trees, her head lowered and eyes glaring. We watched this curious scene for about twenty minutes, finally calling Dixie to the porch.

We were used to seeing them play together, sometimes for hours, but this was different. Dee immediately relaxed but kept a watchful eye on both us and the dog. It eventually became clear what she was doing. Dee obviously had a fawn in those trees and was defending it. Her posture and ears said it all. Keeping herself between us and the fawn made sure it stayed there lying tight to the ground and safe. April even walked slowly toward the trees and although she did not alert on this, Dee still kept herself between April and, most likely, her tiny fawn.

A few weeks later, Delilah brought her baby, tall and healthy, to the back yard to show her off. The little spotted doe was a beautiful, perfect image of her mom and, not surprisingly, our eyes became wet with pure pride and joy. *This* is why we do it.

We never gave Dee's daughter a name and as far as we know she has grown into a proud and fertile mama herself. Deer change colors, so unless there is a distinguishing mark or scar, it is extremely difficult to identify them once they

are in the wild for a few months.

In the past four years, we have seen Dee with five other deer including two bucks who may or may not be her sons. Dee was our first and without a doubt will always be our all-time favorite white tailed deer.

At the writing of this manuscript in August 2020, Dee had been obviously very pregnant. She was moving slowly and her eyes said she was miserable. Standing six feet from her, I could see her unborn fawn pushing against her abdomen. Still, every day at sundown she and her yearling twins would slide out of the woods to feed on the corn and apple slices April puts out. While grazing, her swollen udder forced her into a cute but pitiful waddle. During that quiet time just before dark, Dee waddled silently back to her bedding place in the forest, patiently waiting for the imminent birth and relief from her burden.

Then two days passed and Dee didn't show. You'd think that after experiencing this so many times before, I would just stay calm and simply enjoy the anticipation. I do enjoy those things but deep inside I worry like a parent on prom night.

But on the third day, a gorgeous senior doe, a shadow-gray doe who has obviously lost weight and gained new dignity, emerged from the tree line. Dee's steps were light and proud as she again took her rightful place in the middle of the feed yard.

Our precious Delilah had given birth for the sixth time! Her eyes were bright and she stepped higher, like a proud mom should. Her udder was wet and shrinking, a sure sign that somewhere close by our newest *grandfawn* lay silently awaiting its turn at life in the forest. In a few days or weeks we knew Dee would bring it into the feed yard and here we'd go again. Our place of peace will have one (or two) more blessings.

A month or so later, as we were putting the final edits on the manuscript of this book, in mid-September 2020, we had a very special evening. Delilah came by with the *whole* family and we finally got to meet this year's grandfawns. Delilah had twins *again*. They are strong, healthy and beautiful. The bigger of the two is a male, we believe, with huge ears. We've named him Donkey. The family is comprised of Delilah, Clyde, her son from last year, and his twin sister Bonnie, Delilah's twins from this year, and Shadoe who we raised last year. The whole family was here just before this book went to press!

We began our rehabbing endeavors in the spring of 2013. In the fall of 2015, at the close of a highly active rehabbing year, April recorded the release of a *whopping* sixty-four native animals back into their natural home. It was a busy, satisfying, but very heartbreaking year. We had lost a few babies, due mostly to preexisting conditions. Broken bones, infected wounds, predator bites and dehydration being among ailments our charges endured before arrival.

This was the time that we learned our most valuable lesson: We had clearly taken on more creatures than we should have. The animals we did accept suffered because the two of us could not give the proper time, attention, and care to each of them. The day was too short and the work was almost overwhelming. We vowed never to repeat that mistake and sat down that very night and made a "Capacity Chart" for the next year. We still go by it.

When we manage our numbers, our energy level is up, our attitude is greatly improved, and the animals are much better off, learning more in-depth about how to be wild again. We all learned and everyone won. We must use common sense and learn to say *enough*. Our hearts crack a little when we must refer caring people, who have the best intentions, to other rehab facilities. We will continue to help nature as we can, which is the part we love.

One mild autumn afternoon, April was on our back pathway leading to the woods after checking the field camera for photos of night feeders. As she turned to come back out of the woods, a fully antlered seven-point buck was staring straight at her. She recognized him (I have NO idea how) and called his name, Ernest, a fawn we had rehabbed and released a previous year.

He stopped, ears at half-mast and nose twitching. April took a vanilla wafer from her pocket and slowly held it out and began whistling her Christmas carol! With his ears straight forward and curious, this big boy in velvet trotted to nearly within two feet, then one foot, nosing the cookie, and slipping his lips over it. He raised his proud head and stared directly and deeply into April's eyes.

When I left them, she was scratching his antlers and pulling off dead velvet. Ernest had his eyes closed.

We enjoy what we do immensely, though now we try to temper our attachment to them, knowing that in just a few short months this joy will be replaced by empty enclosures with only the echoes of nature's little miracles.

Lancelot

One fawn that came to us had been the victim of a car accident that killed his Mom and broke his right front leg. A spunky little guy who fully cooperated and was calm during the medical exam, the shots and finally his makeshift cast.

Due to this leg injury, he wore the cast for six weeks. Someone forgot to tell him he was temporarily disabled and he darted around the enclosure with the energy and spunk of any other buck fawn. His little leg poked out in front of him like a jouster's lance. April named him Lancelot. He was as affectionate as he was rambunctious. Lance jumped, strutted, and darted to April at every feeding, always licking her first before his bottle feeding.

After six weeks in a cast, he had adjusted to it quite well and had no trouble running with his roommates. At the end of the sixth week, we removed his cast and Lancelot temporarily lost his mind! He walked nowhere! He bounced everywhere and strutted and tossed his head with pure unadulterated joy! Without a doubt, Lance was our happiest buck. We released him and his mates each morning for their daily browse and he was always first out, last in at night. He playfully head butted and pushed at any other animal that came near him. Lancelot was truly alive. A live wire, as they say.

One evening after April had fed the other babies and was whistling her feeding tune to bring in Lance and his group, we noticed Lance wasn't in his usual big hurry to be fed. Upon close examination, April discovered that his left eye was… gone. Somehow Lance had run through something sharp and his entire eye had been punctured and pulled out. He was obviously in great pain and was limping as well. At this age he was much too big to crate for a trip to the vet and too strong for us to pin him down for treatment. His breathing was labored as well. After agonizing over what to do next, we made the toughest decision any rehabber must make. That night we tearfully put our precious, one-of-a-kind Sir Lancelot out of his misery and into the peaceful beyond.

Lancelot will always have a special place in our heart and memory. We had a hand-carved cedar plaque made with his name on it and it still hangs beside the fountain in our backyard. Walking by the fountain I cannot help but smile at the precious memories of the feisty little buck with three good legs and a joyful manner. There is no single group of animals that touch us. Each one is an individual with a unique personality and needs.

Woody

Woody was the youngest fawn we received, being only one-day old when he came around. He was a very weak, quiet little buck and his umbilical cord was just beginning to dry up. He was a golden colored buck with glaring white spots, weighing less than four pounds and standing no more than fourteen inches tall, with the classic fawn look, like one of those you see in cartoons. We had a feeling that he hadn't received the needed colostrum from his mother's milk, something that aids immunity, before she was hit by a car. With injections of antibiotics, Woody fought and gained a little weight.

After about a week, the antibiotics wore off and his health began to decline. After several weeks of this roller coaster health condition, Woody's little body began to reject even the antibiotics. The decision to end this cycle was made after he could no longer stand and suckle. Our vet was consulted and Woody was injected one final time.

There are times, sitting quietly on our back porch, that his memory will return to us and bring a smile and a tear, because nature has lost a precious creature.

Dolly

The fond memories far outweigh the sad ones, which keeps us doing whatever it takes to aid our local creatures on their way back to the wild. One of the fawns we rehabbed came to us from a nearby upscale neighborhood where deer regularly feed in pristine backyards. Naturally, many roads crisscross this feeding area and we received a call about a newborn whose mother had been another victim of traffic. This little girl was cradled in the curve of her dead

mother's neck.

We named her Dolly and she was the tiniest fawn we have ever encountered. I had never seen a fawn quite like her. Her coat was a dull gray with dull white spots and she weighed in at barely three pounds. Since she was so tiny, she was kept in our bathroom for close observation. For two weeks, our bathroom was her domain and she loved it. Dolly chose a corner for her bed. In front of her were two rolls of toilet paper, side by side. She was so small that these rolls hid her face as she sat behind them. Not so small, though, was her energy level and confidence. Nowhere was safe from Dolly's nose and/or mouth. Licking at anything within reach and standing on her hind legs if it wasn't, caused some drastic rearrangement in the bathroom. Shaver wires, hand towels and toothpaste were particular favorites and had to be moved or secured in a drawer.

Dolly was eventually moved to her outdoor enclosure. None too soon for me. You would have thought we had released a kangaroo out there. Bouncing from corner to corner, side to side, she was hilarious as she burnt off the pent-up energy her vitamin packed formula had produced.

Watching Dolly and her adopted siblings became one of our favorite evening

pastimes. As the summer evenings became cooler, the babies frolicked and jumped over each other, bumped each other and generally created a hilarious jumble of streaking, spotted flashes across the enclosure.

Dolly usually instigated these sessions and was the last one to settle down. The cute little brat was also the first at the bottle-feeding rack!

Dolly and her mates were released from their enclosure into the forest after three months and continued to visit our yard (even after full rehab and release). Through the seasons she has remained energetic and though she is still the smallest of her group, continues to throw her weight around as the undisputed leader of her small group of grown does. She showed up last year, plainly pregnant, and we celebrated with her. So far, we haven't seen her or her fawn but the year, for them, has just started. I expect to see Dolly just any day now. Be safe, Little Lady.

We have rehabilitated more fawns than I can recall here, but they all are recorded in our archives. Some animals, like some people, just stand out in our recorded memory.

We have used this feeding device we ingloriously dubbed "The Titty Bar" for four years now and it's a real back saver when you're feeding so many squirmy fawns. This was designed by my friend, Keith Daniel, and me. The bottles lock in from the back of the feeder because these li'l orphans can get rough at feeding time. It worked so well that on April's request, I made a smaller version of it for the raccoons.

Story 3

Sparky The Kestrel

There have been several unusual critters that we have cared for, and Sparky, a fledgling kestrel, will surely be remembered as one of our favorites.

Sparky came to us from a nearby community veterinarian. Kestrels are small raptors related to hawks. He stood about six inches high, with steel blue eyes and that deep forehead of an eagle. Most of his body was blue with streaks of brown along his sides. We were simply to feed and "bird sit" him for a couple of weeks while the doctor was away on vacation.

I had had very little experience with raptors, and April had even less. So naturally, she accepted and we were fostering a fledgling kestrel. Sparky was a majestic bird. Even though he was tiny, about the size of a red-breasted robin, his personality was the size of a hawk.

April brought home bucket after bucket of live crickets from our local bait shop and Sparky loved them! We moved his birdcage outside one day, after he had been with us for about a week. April would stand near him with his door open and he soon jumped from his cage perch to her hand, where she held the cricket. After several days of this training, Sparky was soon flying all over the yard, landing in trees and watching whatever young birds watch. He became so used to being free that his cage was left open and he only went in for a sip of water now and then during the day. He roosted high in our backyard cedar trees at night.

From a cedar limb overhead, he would flutter his wings and scream his chirp to be fed as soon as April walked into the back yard. On the railing of the back porch, we erected a landing perch covered in leather. In a single day, Sparky learned to land on this perch, where he would scream directly into our ears for a cricket. This got him his treat pretty darn quickly. Sparky was a joy to watch as he soared above our roof, and his dive for his landing arm or perch was breathtaking! His only bad habit was landing on the ground to catch crickets, grasshoppers and anything that moved. This is where cats and dogs roam, so we discouraged his

ground scavenging by scaring him off it.

Late one afternoon our neighbor knocked on the front door and told us we needed to get to his barn across the road quickly. Sparky was chirping wildly and seemed to be hurt. Once inside the barn and following his chirp, we discovered him on a hay bale. Blood was in his wings and streaked along his little head. It was evident…our little Sparky had had a run in with a barn cat. On the ground. Dammit. By the time we got him back across the road, he was gone.

This was one of our most painful losses. We must recall Sparky fondly, though, or the hurt will take over and end our rehabbing days. There are other critters out there that need help. This thought must be our primary goal.

Story 4

"Babs" the Rooster

It's very unusual for us to take in a domestic animal, since most of their ailments are handled by the owner or a vet. A young couple contacted us in the spring of 2015 with what we thought was the weirdest request yet (at the time). They had found an incredibly young chicken beside the road that led directly to a poultry slaughterhouse. No other homes were anywhere close. This chick had fallen off a truck on the way to slaughter.

Somewhere along this pitiful journey something had gone delightfully wrong. As the truck was loaded or jostled, something broke, her door fell open and she tumbled to the truck bed then into a honeysuckle vine. And that's where the sweet couple found her flapping in the bushes, scared but alive.

Holy crap. We simply couldn't refuse such an obviously lucky bird. Even if she was "just a chicken." Babs, as we named her, was delivered the next day in a box. We guessed her age at approximately six weeks old. A solid white chubby body with a way oversized breastbone, scruffy and yellowed from feather dust but otherwise pretty sound. There was, however, an even bigger issue, as we soon found out.

We carried her into the back yard for evaluation. As April gently placed her on the lawn for the first time, we made a horrible discovery: Babs couldn't walk. That's right, she could not walk. This young bird had never stood straight up or walked a single step in the six weeks she'd been alive. Babs had been born in an incubator, transferred to a shoebox-sized cage after that, then fed until her body filled up the cage. She had never touched the ground.

None of that seemed to matter to Babs. After her initial fright, her instincts kicked in and her whole attitude changed. It was as close as I have ever come to watching a chicken scream with delight. She threw her head down to peck at the clover and tumbled, butt over beak, onto her back. With the help of gentle hands showing her how to sit up, she was soon nibbling at the first grass she had ever tasted. It took quite a few lessons but eventually, Babs could hobble along with the rest of our flock.

Just a simple-looking white hen, she never did get any prettier, and it seemed her single talent was simply her will. She never gave up on trying to be like the others. She tumbled, she fell, but she never quit trying to fly, jump, and even clean her feathers.

Babs, as I may have mentioned, was not a very attractive chick. The drugs in her feed had caused her breast area to be greatly oversized, one wing never worked properly and her legs were misshapen. This gave her a slow, ambling, crippled gait, one wing hanging down like a gunfighter, ready to draw.

Each evening, all our charges are fed and settled in. This includes enticing the chickens in the coop for the night, using a bowl of feed and treats. Babs caught on quickly, most evenings. After Babs had been with us for a few months, a routine became established. This one evening though, she was the last one left for the coop and was avoiding it.

I watched as her white body stiffened, her neck went up and out and from her mouth I heard the most horribly garbled rooster crow of my entire life! Have you ever heard a trailer bottom out while going over a railroad crossing? Yeah, that kind of sound. I looked up at April. She was looking at Babs, her jaw hanging open as wide as mine. Babs was a damn *rooster!?*

We finished the feeding chores with stomachs sore from laughing, heads full of surprise, and of course, new name possibilities.

Now I'm no expert, but I know the difference between hens and roosters as well as the next person. This chicken had no rooster comb, no long tail feathers, no enlarged red wattles, or any other rooster trait. This rooster was messed up.

So, Babs became *Bob*—Bob the proud, Bob the gunslinger—who didn't realize how different he was, and I doubt it would have mattered anyway.

But old Bob also had no idea just how ugly that sound he made was. This poor rooster had been thru a lot, we thought. We understood. He had issues. But then that awful-sounding crow started. And Bob loved to screech this painful dagger of a noise at ungodly times, for instance, 2:30 a.m.

This crowing phase of Bob's lasted only a couple of months and then late one night it hit me; I hadn't heard Bob crow in a while. Stepping outside and scanning the coop with my flashlight, I saw all was well and went back to bed. Bob was fine but never crowed again. I don't know, but looking back, I wondered if his system had been sped up or altered so he would age faster, which would explain the end of his crowing. Better living through chemistry?

Bob finally grew an enormous wattle but never a tail bigger than a hen. He followed April everywhere and soon was photo *Bobbing* every event we tried to capture on camera.

He would rush to the backyard at feeding time, wobbling from side to side and April would shout, "C'mon Bob, Wobble that Wattle!" Bob was almost an affectionate rooster. He loved it when April petted his wattle, and sat at her feet whenever she played flute in the backyard.

Bob gained weight, scampered along with the flock for a rich and full two years. He should have been someone's dinner long ago but through simple fate and his luck, Bob strolled around acres of freedom. He lost the use of his legs eventually, then his wings. After watching his walk turn into a stumble and feeding became a painful-looking peck at the ground, it became clear that Bob was suffering.

Finally, when our Rooster named Bob could no longer lift his head to feed, neither of us could bear his starving slowly to death. So sadly, we humanely ended Bob's suffering. But the spirit of this delightfully odd rooster lives in our fond memories.

Story 5

Stewy The Ram

The only other domestic animal we have rehabbed up to now was a quiet and gentle Shetland sheep ram. Our friends, Herb and Sasha, had discovered a full-grown ram wandering in their yard. They asked around but couldn't find anyone to claim him.

So our friends called *us*, describing his condition as horrendous. We had no real choice but to try to help. When I first saw him, I knew why he looked the way he did: He hadn't been sheared in at

least three years. His wool was long, matted and *filthy.* His walk was stiff legged and slow, every step a painful hair-pulling experience. Herb had tried to cut through the hardened wool, but had made only a little progress.

We easily slipped a rope over his full-circle horns and led him to our truck. He hardly kicked at all as three of us slid him into the carrier I prayed would hold him should he decide to escape. Luckily for us, he simply laid down for the entire trip back home.

His name came to us on the way home as we joked about lamb stew. That was shortened and this monstrous ball of wool became Stewy, our first and only Shetland sheep.

It took four people hours upon hours to cut through the layers upon layers of hardened wool. And we barely made a difference.

Stewy could not even get away from his poop, his wool was so long and tangled. It had simply collected in a pocket beneath his rear and it was full. The smell was extremely foul and eye burning.

We reached out on social media for a sheep shearer. A wonderful couple from South Tennessee answered our request and drove to us! These kind folks had sheep of their own and he had been shearing for years. He refused to let us pay him. Donations like this are priceless.

After several of us had sawed and cut clumps of Stewy's wool, starting at the neck, the shearer started slicing, the "plates" of old hardened wool away in ragged

sheets. Two hours later, Stewy stood up and a completely different ram had taken his place. He wasn't very big at all and his eyes had brightened into a smile. A knee-deep pile of disgusting wool scrap lay beside him. Stewy was free to move and move he did. He bucked, jumped, and squirmed like an oversized lamb! We kept Stewy for a few months in his own private pasture, to fatten him up and make sure he was recovered. As usual, he fell in love with April and was very protective of her. Even our dogs weren't allowed to approach her when Stewy was nearby. The few times they did, his head went down and Stewy went into full charge mode, never once bluff charging. No pup was ever hurt but that was because they are pretty fast dodgers.

Finally, this chubby and healthy "Stewy the Ram" was donated to a small sheep farm as part of their breeding stock. He gets regular grooming, acres to roam and his choice of cute ewes every day. You're da head Ram, Stewy, from rag to riches!

Story 6

Baby Flying Squirrels

It is profoundly understood by every good rehabber that inarguably the *best* action in the case of a wild baby alone on the ground, is to reunite the baby with mom.

This may be as simple as watching a fawn lie next to a pasture fence, seemingly abandoned. The mother does roam far and wide grazing and, sometimes, may roam a little too far. Not owning wristwatches, they may be away from the fawn for as long as two days.

For years rehabilitators have tried to dispel the old wives' tale that animal mothers will abandon their baby if handled by humans. I can't stress enough that this is NOT the case…ever. Any baby moved to a nearby safer spot will still be accepted by the mother, even with the smell of human on its body.

I can't document every call we get, but I can tell you we have had hundreds of "no action needed" reunion calls — birds, squirrels, deer. These are our *most* gratifying rehab adventures.

As we stood outside our neighbor's woodshop one chilly spring morning, his cat dropped a mousey looking pinky baby at my feet. Field mice abound around us, so this was my thought at first glance.

I moved it with my foot and it opened its arms to reveal two flaps of skin running from the front of each leg to the rear one. "Holy sheesh! Y'all look at this," I stammered, picking up this tiny furless flying squirrel. Its pinhead-sized eyes were tightly closed, naked little arms flailing the air.

Examination showed no wounds or punctures. No broken limbs. As we looked around, the cat ran about twenty-five yards up a trail to a tall, skinny cedar tree. We had no better ideas, so we followed the cat to the tree. High in that thin cedar was a pair of jeans blown up there, no doubt, by some hard, past winter winds. As we looked around for a possible nest, we all saw it at the same time. From the torn knee of those jeans peeked two tiny eyes, the mom!

Elated, we threw together a nest box from a plastic bowl and washcloth. Lining that with straw and cotton we placed the baby into this downy little nest. Keith, our tall neighbor, wired this to the tree trunk. All of us then quietly backed away with the *rescue* cat held securely in the neighbor's arms.

We'd quietly chatted for about ten minutes, when we saw her silently sliding down the trunk of the cedar until she reached the bowl. Sniffing a few times, she took her baby in her mouth and climbed back up the tree. Safely back in the jeans, she still wasn't done.

That day we also got the bonus of watching a mother flying squirrel fly from one tree to a new nest in another, twice, each time with a little one aboard! I suppose she just didn't feel safe in the old nest anymore.

So, you see? Gotta *LOVE* these kinds of lessons.

We never saw the flyers after that but then, that wasn't the point. Helping when you can, just for the sake of helping, expecting nothing in return. The irony is those little flyers gave us both a story and an amazing adventure.

Story 7

Elsa The Bobcat

Elsa came to us as a tiny one-pound bobcat kitten. Her mother had been shot. Elsa showed up a day later in a neighbor's barn, hungry and cold. A fluffy, spotted, dirty-brown coat covered her scrawny little back and belly. Elsa's eyes were large and golden yellow and never missed a single movement. We named her Elsa in honor of the lioness in the heartwarming book *Born Free* by Joy Adamson. She took to formula and thrived with regular feedings and warm cleanings, like her mom had done. Mostly she slept on top of her nest box during the warm spring days. Unless, of course, she heard our footsteps coming around

the nursery to her.

Many times we looked in at her, seeing nothing, scanning the enclosure in all the places she should have been. But we learned to be still, to move only our eyes. Then we'd catch the twitch of her tail and following it up we could see a splayed-out Elsa, crouched right at our feet, almost invisible with her tawny coat and her stillness.

Around this time, we had to renew our rehab permit and our facility was inspected by a state conservation officer. She was a very courteous, professional woman who strolled around, making few notes but observing every enclosure. When we came to Elsa's enclosure she stopped, looked around a bit and finally asked, "Did you say you had a bobcat here? May I see it?"

I smiled and pointed at the ground just inside the enclosure. There, two feet away, Elsa gazed up at her, frozen into a stalk, with only her tail twitching. We laughed and all agreed that a bobcat's camouflage is absolutely amazing.

Of course, she and April adored each other. From the first night's bottle feeding, as I watched Elsa and April look into each other's eyes, I could see a bond forming between those two ladies.

Elsa was wonderful but could be savage, April reminisces about this amazing creature. *Feeding alone was an adventure. I had to sneak in a chicken wing on a long stick through the wire of the door and she would attack it like a lion to a gazelle. Then while she was occupied with the wing, I slipped her food dish into her enclosure. She could and would have taken my hand off. Playtime was fun but usually drew blood. She was alone. Although I do not encourage play between human*

and animal because it creates too much bonding, Elsa needed company and interaction to a certain degree.

We had our quiet moments, too. She loved to gently paw my finger as she suckled the baby bottle. Or after feeding, I relished her warmth on my neck as she slipped off to sleep.

We decided it was time to give her a try at wildness life and sadly released her a respectable distance from her birth but, not so sadly, she found her way back to us within two weeks.

I got up early one morning and saw a strange cat pacing back and forth at the fawn enclosure. It took me a few minutes to realize it wasn't just any cat…it was Elsa the Bobcat. I called her and she came running to me, jumped into my arms, and tried to eat my fingers. She was thin and hungry but strong and full of energy. I finally had to pin her down, grab her by the nape and put her back in her enclosure.

We kept her for another month. She was obviously able but still a little too immature for release. No doubt she would have slaughtered a fawn that day, had I not seen her in time."

During the last month, Elsa grew like a weed and her movements smoothed from those of a slightly jumpy kitten into the graceful, muscular flow of a powerful, very-able huntress.

Finally, at five months old, we released our beloved Elsa beside a wildlife preserve where rabbits and squirrels and other rodents thrive. This time though, we drove several miles away to make sure she stayed free. Elsa remains wild and I'm sure the Queen of her forest.

Story 8

Red Foxes

Red foxes are nasty, y'all. In the wild, they move about constantly, so wherever they stand becomes a toilet. Usually odor is no problem. Unless the fox is confined. This, folks, presents a problem. Not to the fox, he will still relieve himself wherever he stands. Nest box, water dish, food dish, you name it. Did I mention the rancid, gut-wrenching smell of red fox poop?

And extremely destructive. You almost wish for food dishes made of titanium because they will bite, tear and destroy every bed, blanket, plastic toy—anything that fits in their mouth—and crap on it, too, of course.

We have rehabbed a total of nine as of this writing and plan to do as few as possible from now on. We have, however, had a few fun adventures with two different species of foxes.

Dandy was a red fox kit found huddled in a drainage ditch after a hard rain. She had been in the ditch the entire day, according to the concerned lady. She

walked up to the food that was offered her and slipped right into a pet carrier and was dropped off at our cabin.

She immediately bonded to April, to the surprise of no one. Dandy weighed about two pounds, and after a warm bath, her blazing red hair glistened and stood out, making her appear twice that weight. The first night we had her she slept in the bathroom, in a crate. The next morning, she hungrily fed from a bottle and nibbled at everything else. We moved her into a large, outdoor enclosure, after a thorough physical exam for parasites. Nervous at first, she ran around the perimeter and finally cowered in a corner and yep—squatted and peed.

Dandy settled in very quickly though, eventually running up to April every time she came near. Crawling on her chubby tummy she would whine, wag her little tail, and flatten her ears begging for food or attention. At feeding time Dandy would approach April at a crawl, ears laid back and squeaking for the bowl of food in April's hands. This almost chubby little kit was fed raw meat, apples and nuts.

Dandy's play activities were sporadic throughout the day, at times just sniffing the enclosure wire from top to bottom. At other times it was jumping through the tire suspended from the ceiling. We supplied toys, short trees and a hammock to keep her entertained.

As she grew, her fur filled out even more and she gained weight. Her bathroom habits, however, never changed. You name it, we tried it: litter box, scolding (ha!), moving poop piles to one spot hoping for a miracle. Nope. Dandy continued to do her business wherever and whenever she chose.

After four months, we released the chubby little girl in a flower-filled meadow beside an oak grove. She walked out of the transport carrier, glanced once at us, and bounced into the woods, happy, healthy, and free.

Dandy was memorable and a joy to rehab in many ways, but I must admit her release was less than tearful.

Story 9

Gray Foxes

Victor and Vixen

Only a few days old, Victor and two siblings were brought to an animal shelter. They looked almost like kittens. When the shelter owner couldn't identify them, she called our state fish and wildlife office and sent them pictures. They were identified as gray foxes.

The shelter owner tried slipping the tiny foxes under a mamma cat, hoping she would adopt and feed them but, sadly, two of the siblings died. After Victor began to get a little rough on the mamma cat, especially at feeding time, they transported the fox kit to us. His age was determined to be three weeks old.

Since he was the only survivor, we named him Victor. We knew he would be difficult to "wild up" because he had never seen foxes…he was raised like a cat. Incredibly agile and curious, Victor was as affectionate as any pup I've

ever known. He was playful and friendly, which is unusual, since the gray fox is known to be more aggressive than his red cousin.

As fate would have it, a couple of weeks later we received Vixen, as we named her. She was another gray fox about a week older and much wilder. She was the perfect sibling for Victor. Vixen had been raised in the wild and left behind when her family had to be relocated from a suburban back yard. She was too young to be on her own but *wild* already, and her instincts were excellent.

In a few short days, the two bonded well, although Victor became the dominant one. Feeding time created snarling squabbles but no one was hurt, Vixen always giving in and cowering beneath Victor. Gray foxes are more omnivorous than the red foxes. They would eat a lot more fruits and vegetables than meat. Both slept in the nest box and lay side-by-side during the daytime heat and played together every evening.

Release time for these kits was special, sad yet extremely satisfying. When they were about six months old, and after they had been with us for five, we planned their return to the wild. We transported the foxes together in a dog carrier and covered it to reduce the stress. In a beautiful meadow lined on one side by a creek and huge cedars along the rest, we gently placed the carrier on the ground and slipped off the covering.

At first, Vixen bolted out but not too far, glancing back for Victor. He was taking his time, playing in the new grass with new smells. Vixen wouldn't just leave without him. I knew he was in good company with her out there in the wild. We stood there quietly, drinking in this once in a lifetime scene that we were so privileged to witness.

Story 10

Groundhogs

Abby

We received a call about a young groundhog who'd been bitten by a dog and now had an eye injury. We have raised a couple of groundhogs, also known as *marmots*, *woodchucks*, and *whistle pigs*, and we knew that they could become extremely aggressive.

After a brief conversation, it was decided that the caller would transport the "adolescent" animal to us. I was surprised to see it barely fit into a plastic tub. She was huge! A full-size adult ground hog.

These folks relayed the sad story that they had found it on the road, but it quickly became evident that was *not* a wild groundhog. This girl was a pet who probably got too close to the dog bowl at feeding time. She was extremely gentle and tolerant of human contact.

At the vet, her injured eye was removed, healed and Abby, as we named her, recovered completely. She was quiet, never made any loud sound. She was always just waiting on dinner or slipping a nut out of April's hand. A wild ground hog

would have snapped her finger off.

It was obvious that this fat girl couldn't be released and other than having her one eye, she was rather fat and healthy. So, we found a solution.

A rehabber in South Alabama was searching for an "unreleaseable" groundhog to be used as an educational animal to show in schools and other events. Abby was perfect for this. We met the rehabber halfway and transferred the groundhog to his care where she lived quite a few years as a pet and educational animal.

Sammy

Another little groundhog girl was Sammy, who came to us as a baby. Sammy was the only survivor of four babies found inside the engine of a tractor. She still had her eyes closed when she arrived and we learned that bottle feeding a groundhog is an adventure. Even when very young, they have sharp teeth and a silicone or rubber nipple on the feeding bottle doesn't last very long. They tend to aspirate and can easily drown, so it is a bit of a wrestling match to bottle feed these little creatures. We went through a lot of nipples.

Groundhogs seem to go from one extreme to the other. They can be very aggressive. But some imprint easily. Sammy was very gentle and friendly. It was hard not to imprint her. She taught us a lot about groundhogs. She was a mentally bright animal and learned survival lessons very well. Once she was

weaned, after we had her about four months, and she could find shelter and was able to eat all kinds of food such as lettuce, nuts and most any garden vegetables, she was ready to go. Her release was easy as caring for her had been. April lifted her from her enclosure into a carrying crate, we drove to a previously chosen release site, opened her crate door and Sammy waddled out. She sat up on her hind legs, looked around, gave a short whistle of approval and was gone. Groundhogs are also not very good at good-byes.

Story 11

Opossums

We have received baby possums from so many situations: car accidents, dog attacks and sometimes sheer abandonment when they fall out of Mom's pouch or off her back. It's hard to share just one. We don't get just one or two opossums. They usually arrive by the half or full dozen and push the rehabbing numbers up.

These guys are quietly misunderstood by many folks. Up until just a few years ago they were considered nasty, pesky varmints that slunk around stealing chicken eggs. Thanks to better education and the internet, we now know they are pretty darn wily and seem to enjoy their role as "Janitors of The Woods". Thanks partly to possums, our forests and woods are odor free. Now don't get me wrong, possums are opportunists, also. From personal experience, I know they will kill roosting chickens at night. Easy solution: pen up your chickens at sundown. Their main diet with us was nuts soaked to soften them, fruits that are overripe, and worms, and so forth.

Possums are very hardy and much cleaner than we ever thought. One nest of three orphans we rehabbed loved to sleep in an old sock hung to side of the enclosure.. As they grew, a bucket lined with clean, old rags made the perfect nest box for teenage to adult possums. A small log mounted from the wall to the floor gave them climbing access to this cuddly new nest.

One day, as we were cleaning, I noticed a little guy with a wad of leaves seemingly stuck to his butt. As I watched he climbed the perch, turned around and relaxed his prehensile tail, dropping the leaves on his nest mates' heads. Inside the bucket, the others began mouthing the leaves and arranging them on the floor and wall of the nest. We watched this scene recur about six or eight times throughout the day and that evening the nest was very well insulated and even more cozy. I had no idea possums did this with their tails.

Opossums are marsupials and nocturnal. This makes them fairly easy to rehab. Well, this and the fact that possums will potty train themselves. Speaking of amazing possum tricks, here's one: If you provide a shallow dish of water somewhere in their enclosure, they will find it and use it as a toilet. Yep. Possums pee in water when they can. April always provides a drip water bottle for drinking, but this shallow pan is so much easier to clean than the entire enclosure! You're welcome.

There is actually no prep required for opossum release; they are reclusive and prefer dark places. At release time, it's just a matter of slipping them into a carrier, then opening the door upon reaching the release site.

Story 12

Dixie

Ever since we have been rehabbers, we have also had personal pets, dogs and cats for our enjoyment and fun. One rule they all obey without question is that the wild animals which April or I have introduced to them are strictly off limits for close contact. That means no barking at them, no running around inviting them to play, and so forth. In short, just ignore them. For the most part we have been lucky and successful with our pets' attitudes.

There is one special story though (isn't there always?). We rescued Dixie, our Doberman-Rottweiler, when she was three months old. With the typical black and tan markings and the build of a Doberman, her eyes will melt you. She has this little wrinkle between her eyes, eyes so brown it's like the color has no bottom.

Dixie is three years old now and continues to be a great and loving assistant and friend. One evening as the mid-spring sun was going down, after some heavy downpours, I stepped outside to call in the dogs. Dixie came trotting slowly up the porch and did not greet me at all, just stood looking at the door. I saw she had something in her mouth. It could be an old cow bone or some other disgusting thing, so I wanted to check it out. No way. Dixie kept her head down and clearly did *not* want me to touch whatever this was. I was completely shocked. She always gave it up when asked. Anything.

But trusting her to have a reason, I gave in. Dixie went straight to her bed and laid down. April came over and we could clearly see that there was something under her. April lifted her and there, wriggling, naked and chirping was a baby opossum! The little guy was maybe two weeks old and had apparently fallen off his mother's back, judging by Dixie's past performance of running off critters that wander onto *her* property.

We were amazed that she had carried this little fella in her mouth through the woods without leaving a single scratch. Think we got a "Rehab Dog" on our hands? We sure like to think so.

After several unsuccessful attempts to reunite him with Mom we took him in. The lucky li'l possum made it through rehab, with Dixie watching his every move when he ventured out of his nest. We released him on the big hill across a pasture from us. Back into his rightful home, the woods.

Dixie continues to amaze us with her desire to please and gentle nature. She is still sniffing and wagging her nubby tail at each new arrival.

Sometimes it isn't just babies, April observes about Dixie. *We had a stubborn hen who wouldn't lay her eggs in the coop and no one knew where she hid her eggs. One mild spring morning as I stepped onto the door mat of the back porch, I was surprised and delighted to find a fresh, clean egg lying at my feet. "What a luxury," I thought to myself, "to have a chicken that not only lays big eggs but delivers them too!"*

The next day, I found another egg on the mat of the FRONT porch. Nope, no way a hen would walk up twelve steps to the front porch to lay her egg. The mystery had begun.

Sure enough, the following day, through the living room window I watched Dixie proudly climbing the front porch with—yep, an egg in her mouth—and placing it gently on the mat. Mystery solved and she got plenty of praise and treats that day.

She never broke or cracked the eggs. They were placed carefully on the mat and she went about her business. So, for weeks, every time I saw the egg, I would leave a treat in its place, like the egg fairy.

Story 13

The Teepee

At some point, forgetting that I was a grown man, I decided I'd like to make a teepee. After hours of searching for materials and even more hours sewing, I constructed what I thought was a fairly good replica of a twelve-foot-high structure in shape of a cone.

It was cozy, and I must admit, toasty warm on chilly spring nights. For some odd reason, our animals loved it as much as we did. An average evening teepee gathering included, two dogs, two cats, a white-tail fawn and us. April would bring out a nursing raccoon occasionally, feeding it from a tiny bottle.

During these times with cooler evenings and full bellies, our critters would get frisky. A special spectacle was Dixie chasing the cats around the teepee, then watching our little doe, Piggy, join in the chase! Piggy would lower her head and charge Dixie, who dodged her easily. Then Dixie would take chase…this went on until almost sundown.

Finally, when the sun began to set and we could see our breath in the frosty

air, Piggy would head slowly off into the woods to join her stepsisters. Often, we would gather the remaining critters inside the teepee and listen to the night animals wake up for their turn at food.

The coyotes yelping, owls hooting from deep in the cedars and the unseen rustling of night hunters, all proving that the forest never sleeps.

Once, when the moon was just right, we saw a full moon straight above us through the smoke hole of the teepee. It was hypnotic the way the clouds floated silently through the light. The teepee poles formed a spiraling frame around the whole scene. It was captivating.

The teepee was a tougher idea than I had thought. Besides being extremely time consuming to build, the material (a lightweight, indoor canvas floor covering for painters) was low quality and, too soon, began to mold and tear at the slightest touch. It collapsed from the top, like an old man whose coveralls are falling. Yes, I had coated it with a sealant for cloth. The inferior material I bought simply wasn't up to the weather. What offset all that to me was how much our family of critters enjoyed it. Still have my poles stored away, so maybe someday…

Story 14

Communication And Patience

Phone calls, though a necessary medium for communication, information, and our main source of acquiring animals, can be amusing and, at times, even scary. These queries can range from a simple question about care and feeding to, "How do I trap a baby bird?" (Don't laugh yet, this isn't the weirdest). We know there are no "stupid" questions but sometimes they can be, let's just say, unusual.

One warm summer evening after the critters had been fed and we were just about to have dinner, of course, the phone rang. I made the mistake of answering instead of returning the call after my meal. The lady on the phone was very pleasant and had a fawn she needed help with.

We chatted about the situation and I deduced that she had inadvertently "kidnapped" the fawn. Her son had found it in a field beside a tree line on their property. He had brought it home and they needed advice on feeding until they could locate a rehabber. I explained that the mom had most likely bedded her baby in the field so she could wander off a bit and graze. The caller explained that they had watched the field the day before and no deer had come to the field.

She went on to explain that her daughter had just had a baby two weeks before. Then the question, "Can she breast feed the fawn?" just shut me up completely. After a long pause and me choking on smothered laughter, I could only whisper, "No, Ma'am."

Taking a few deep breaths and biting my lip, I explained that deer do not wear wrist watches, so they may wander a day or two even, before working their way back to the baby. But they WILL make it back if they are able. She needed to simply put the fawn back where it was found and leave it alone.

To her credit, this loving lady did just that and called us the next morning, proudly stating that the mom had appeared in the field the evening before and the fawn had trotted up to her, nursed and they wandered back into the tree line. You could hear how proud she was! This scenario occurs time and again when folks find babies seemingly abandoned and quiet. A final note: Fawns leave no scent for the first few weeks of life, helping them avoid predators as they lie perfectly still.

The Adventure Continues

As you read this, we are full of this years' orphaned young and each one has its own special tale (pun fully intended). It's as if we get to start all over on a familiar yet brand new adventure. Each new year has presented us with new challenges and never-before-seen circumstances, the same as the previous year did.

I hope you have enjoyed these critter tales and will be inspired to take a walk, or several, into your own woods somewhere. Smile as a squirrel scampers up a tree or a hawk flies over, and you may feel a little sense of adventure that will make your day.

We sincerely thank you for your interest in what we do at Shamballa Wildlife Rescue.

Best,

John Russ

About the Author

John S. Russ was born in Huntsville, Alabama. He grew up with a natural love for nature and animals. He left Alabama to join the Marine Corps in 1966.

After a stint in Vietnam he was transferred to El Toro Marine Air Base, then discharged in 1970. He settled in California where he volunteered for three years at the Wildlife Waystation, nestled in the Angeles National Forest, and later at The Los Angeles Zoo for two more years.

In 2008, he came home to Alabama and shortly after, met his wife April, also a naturalist at heart. Together they became involved in rescuing the local indigenous wildlife. John and April founded Shamballa Wildlife Rescue in 2013 on their small mountain farm in the North Alabama woods.

This is John's first full-fledged attempt at authorship, although his work has been featured in several other publications. When he's not reading or writing, he can be found in the barn with his new best friend, "Humphrey," a one-year-old mini-donkey.

Shamballa Wildlife Rescue

Made in the USA
Columbia, SC
17 October 2024

44276442R00031